Would It Be Right

Does it make sense?

Would it be right?

Would it help others?

Would it stop a fight?

5

These are the things we all must ask

When we first approach a task.

Will it be safe?

Will it be fair?

Will it solve problems?

Does it show you care?

These are the things we all must ask

When we first approach a task.

So wait till you get all the facts.

Think through choices

before you act!